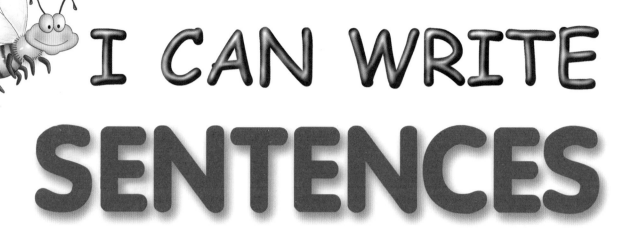

# I CAN WRITE SENTENCES

U0099690

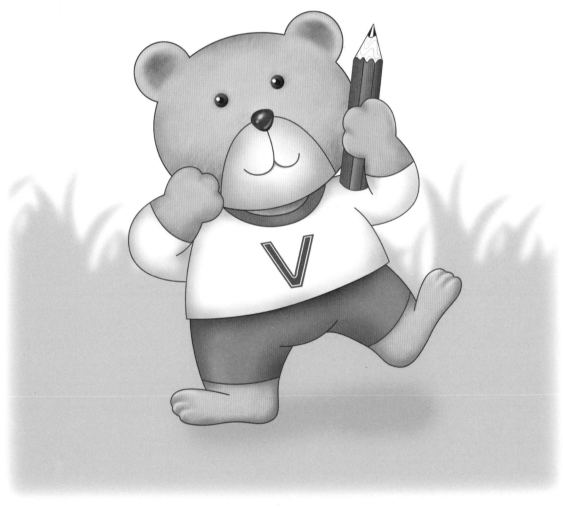

SUN YA PUBLICATIONS (HK) LTD.

www.sunya.com.hk

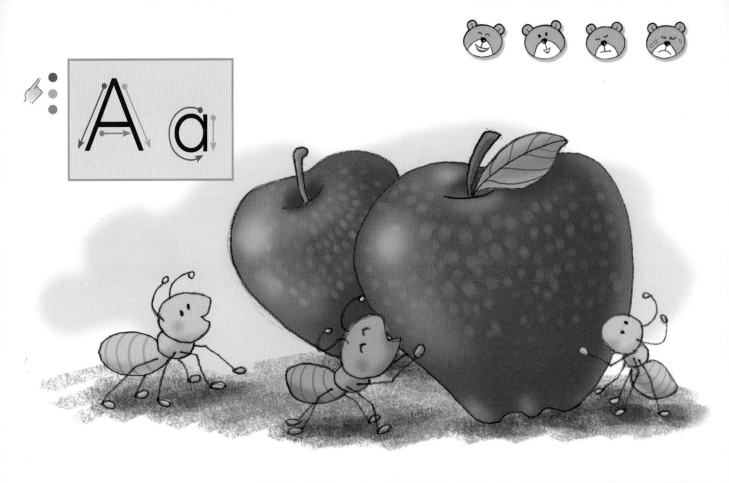

Ants are eating apples.

Ants are eating apples.

Ants are eating apples.

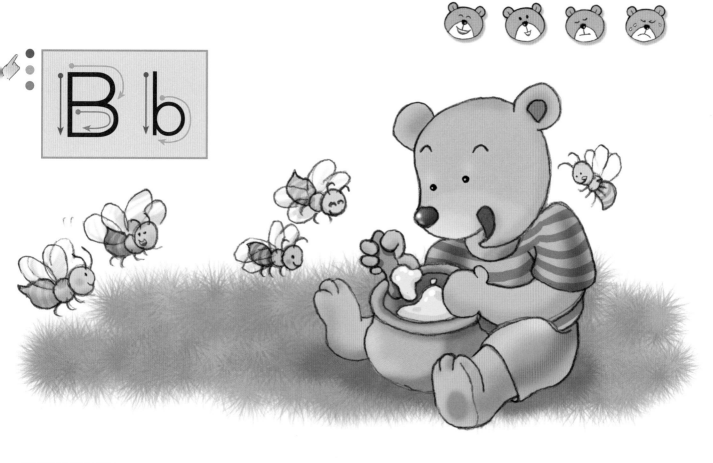

Bees are buzzing around a bear.

Bees are buzzing around a bear.

Bees are buzzing around a bear.

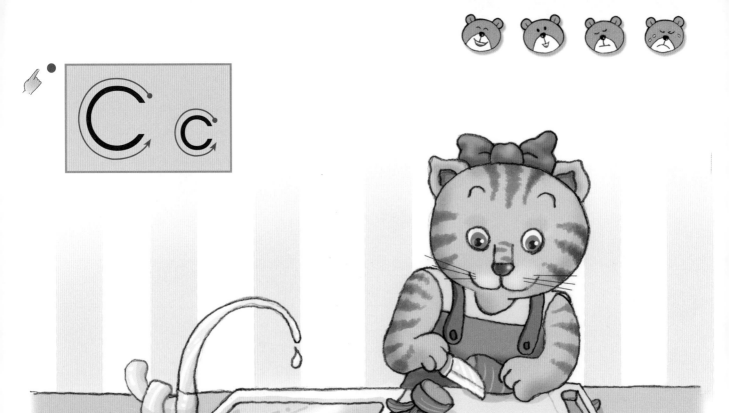

The cat is cutting a carrot.

The cat is cutting a carrot.

The cat is cutting a carrot.

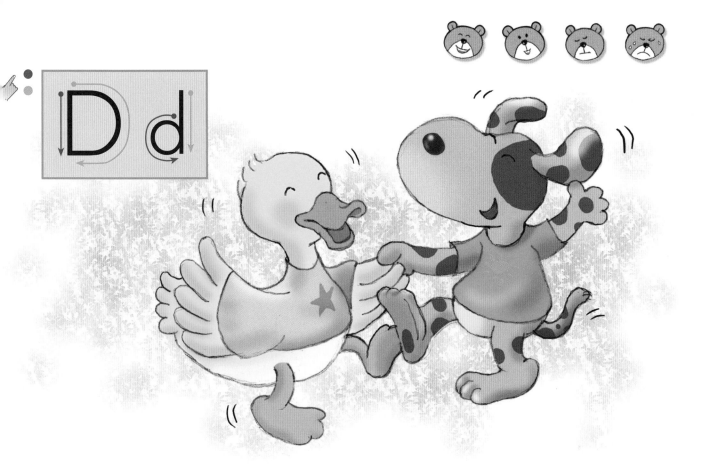

# D d

The dog is dancing with a duck.

The dog is dancing with a duck.

The dog is dancing with a duck.

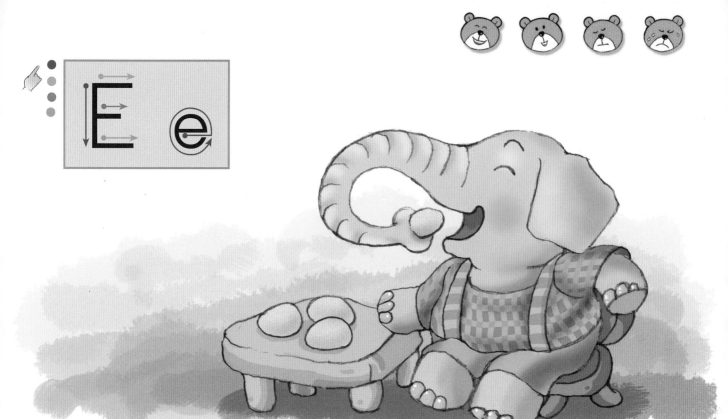

The elephant is eating eggs.

The elephant is eating eggs.

The elephant is eating eggs.

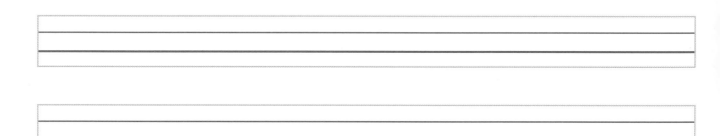

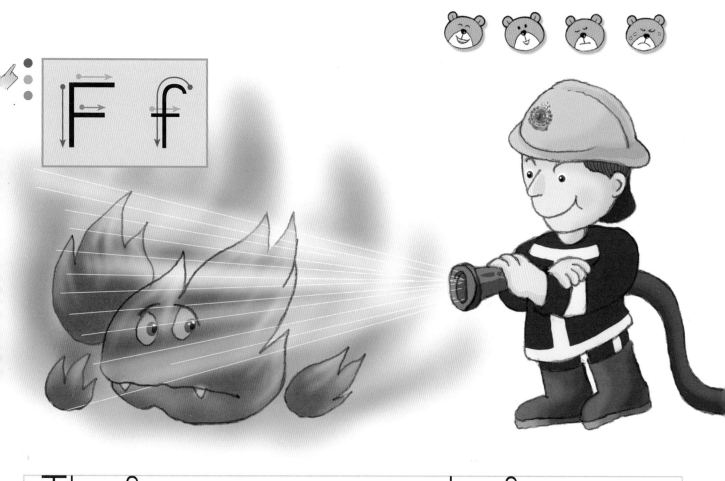

The fireman is putting the fire out.

The fireman is putting the fire out.

The fireman is putting the fire out.

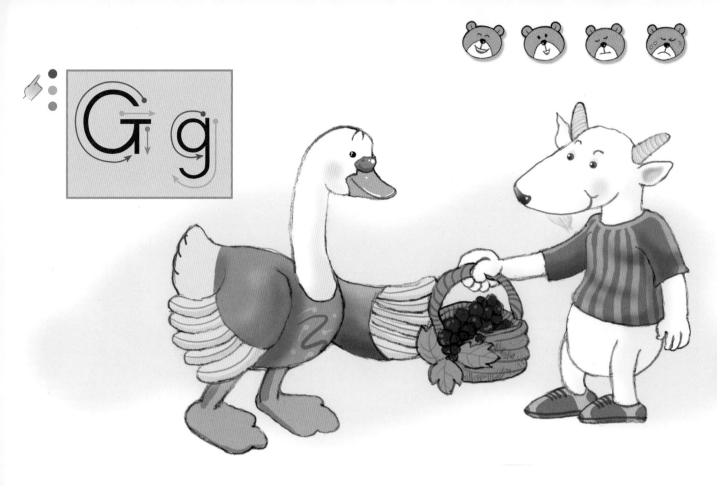

The goat gives the goose some grapes.

The goat gives the goose some grapes.

The goat gives the goose some grapes.

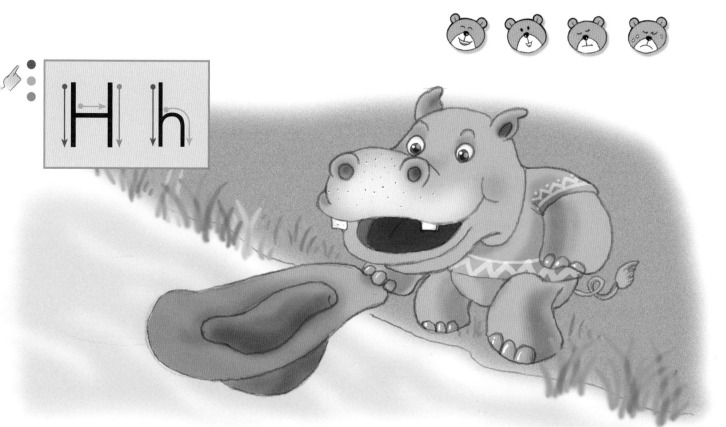

The hippo is washing a hat.

The hippo is washing a hat.

The hippo is washing a hat.

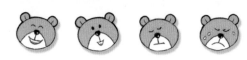

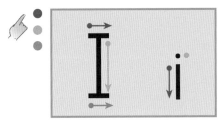

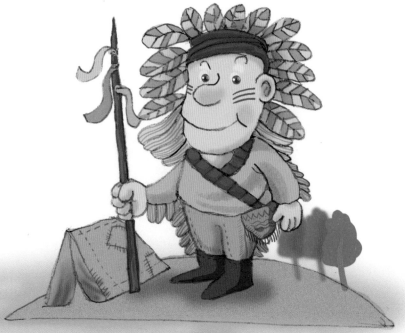

The Indian lives on an island.

The Indian lives on an island.

The Indian lives on an island.

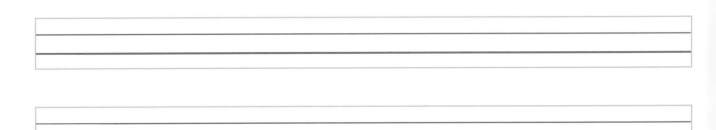

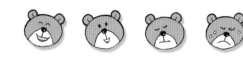

# J j

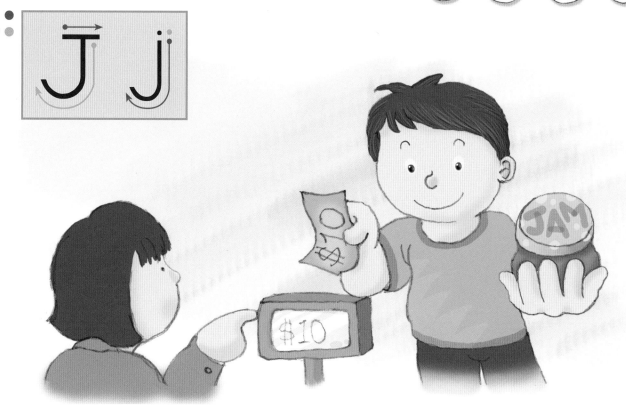

Jack buys a jar of jam.

Jack buys a jar of jam.

Jack buys a jar of jam.

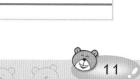

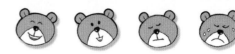

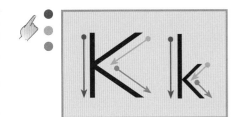

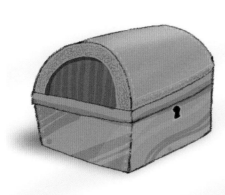

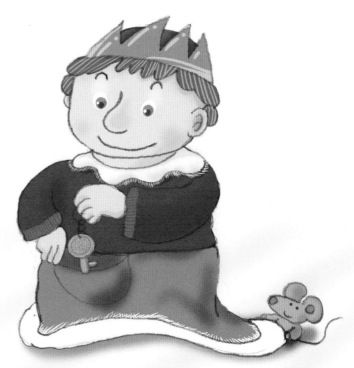

The king keeps the key in his pocket.

The king keeps the key in his pocket.

The king keeps the key in his pocket.

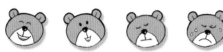

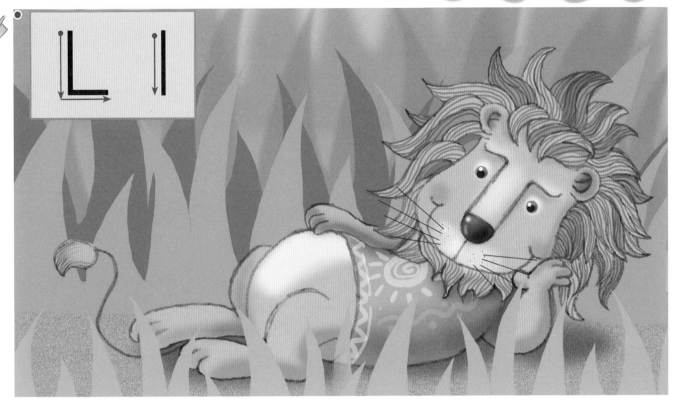

The lion lies in the long grass.

The lion lies in the long grass.

The lion lies in the long grass.

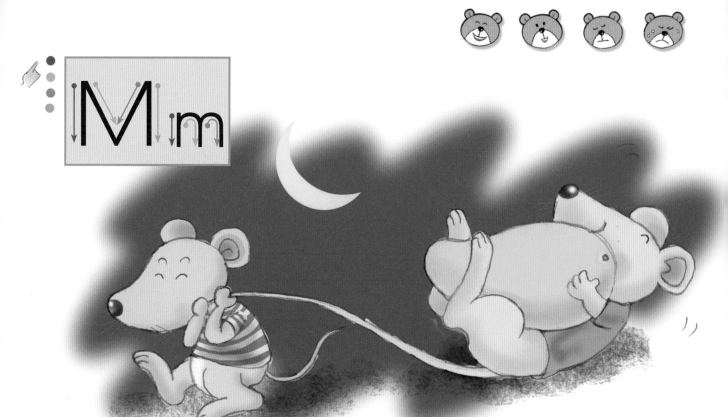

The mice are moving a mango.

The mice are moving a mango.

The mice are moving a mango.

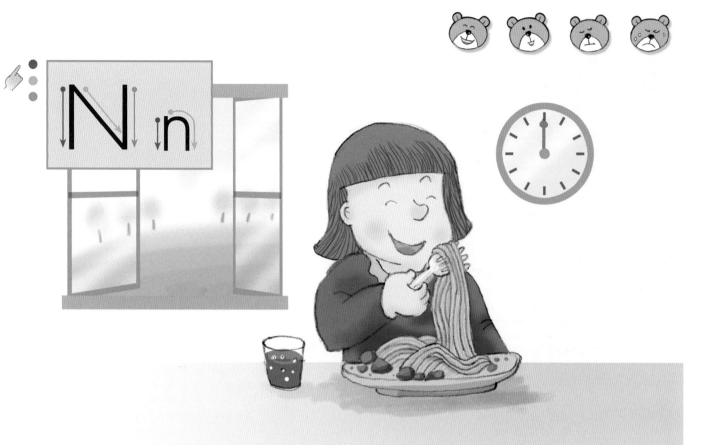

Nancy is having noodles at noon.

Nancy is having noodles at noon.

Nancy is having noodles at noon.

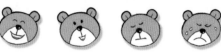

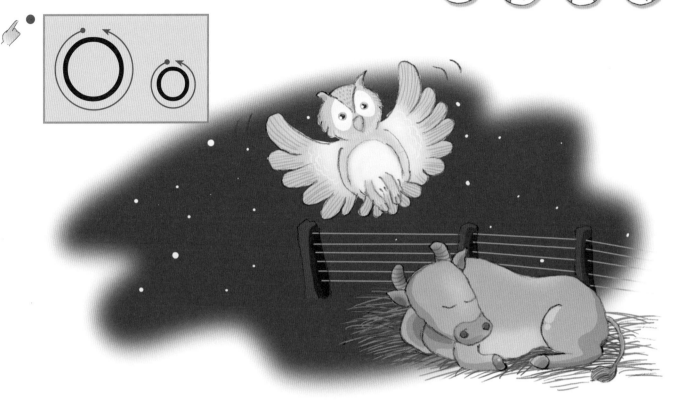

The owl is flying over an ox.

The owl is flying over an ox.

The owl is flying over an ox.

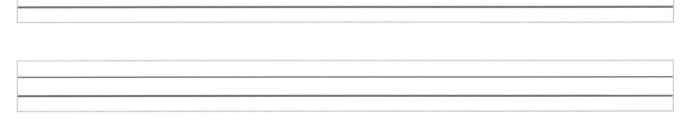

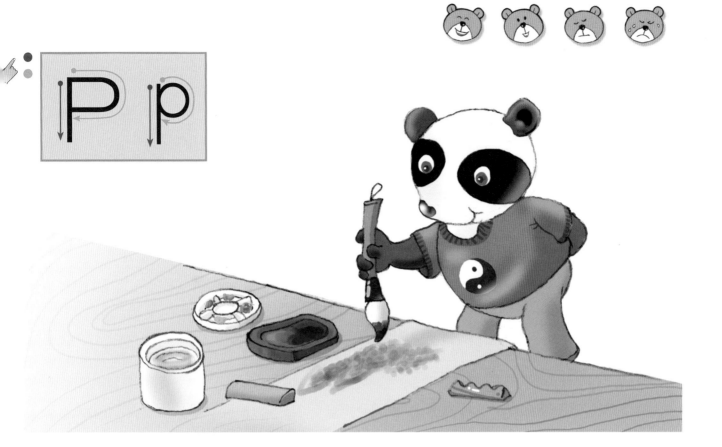

The panda is painting a picture.

The panda is painting a picture.

The panda is painting a picture.

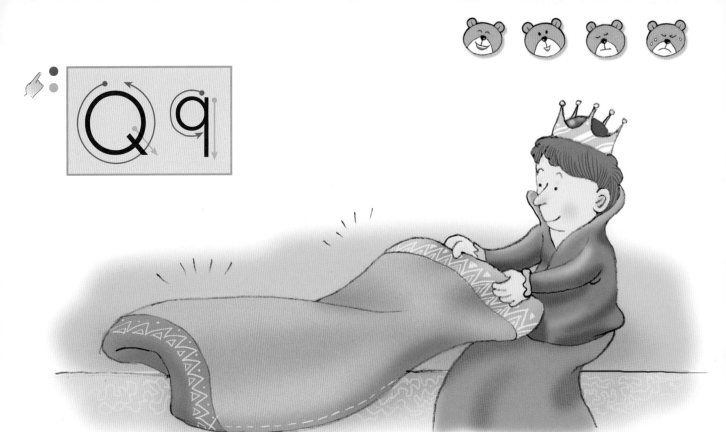

The queen has a new quilt.

The queen has a new quilt.

The queen has a new quilt.

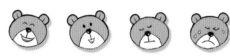

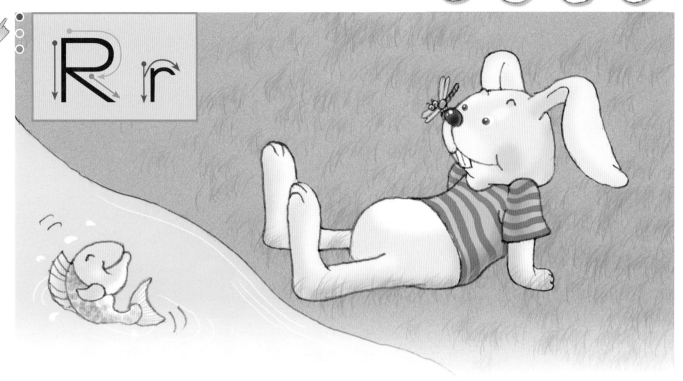

R r

The rabbit rests near the river.

The rabbit rests near the river.

The rabbit rests near the river.

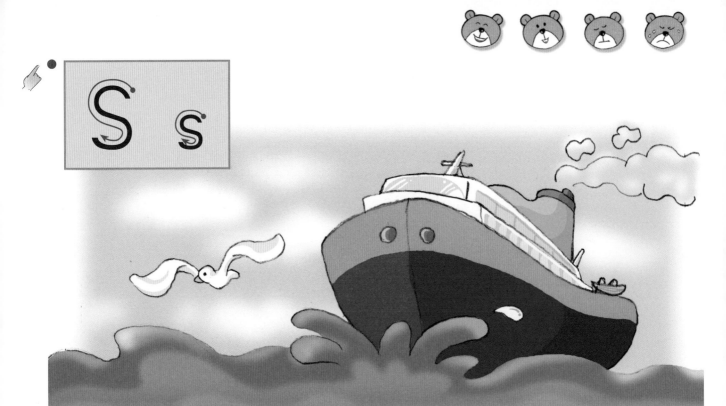

## S s

A ship is sailing on the sea.

A ship is sailing on the sea.

A ship is sailing on the sea.

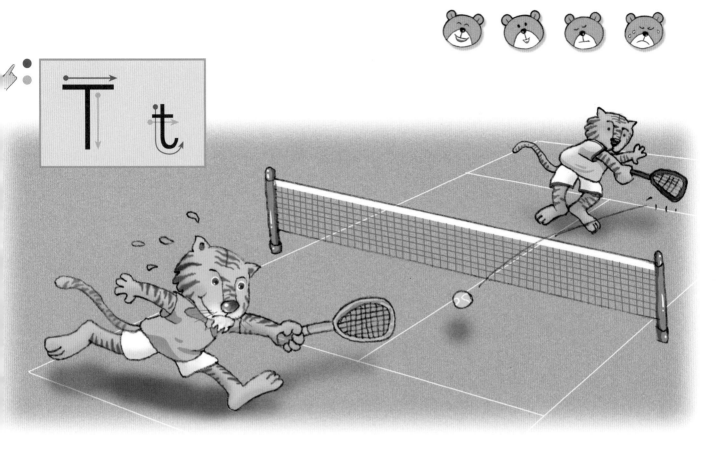

The tigers are playing tennis.

The tigers are playing tennis.

The tigers are playing tennis.

# U u

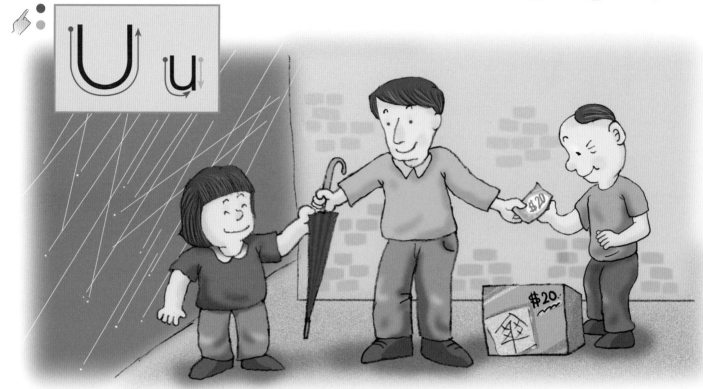

Uncle buys me an umbrella.

Uncle buys me an umbrella.

Uncle buys me an umbrella.

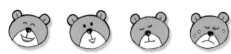

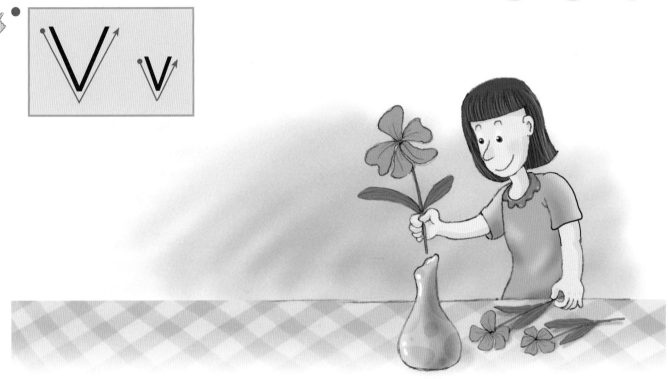

Vicky puts the violets in a vase.

Vicky puts the violets in a vase.

Vicky puts the violets in a vase.

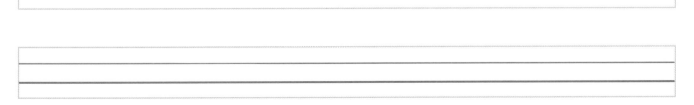

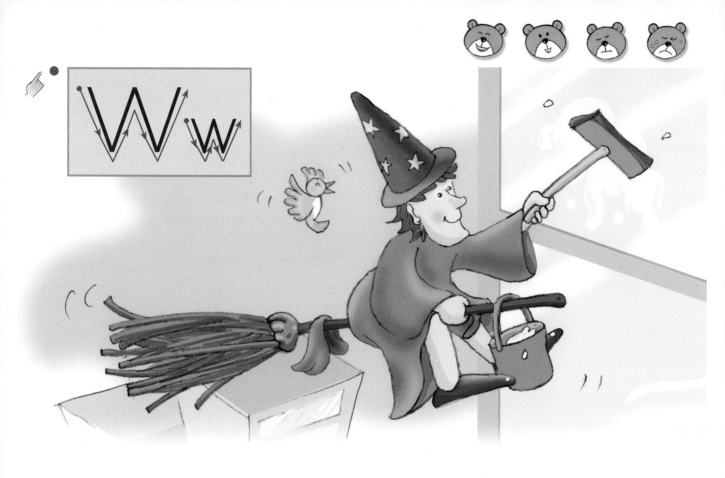

# Ww

The witch is wiping the window.

The witch is wiping the window.

The witch is wiping the window.

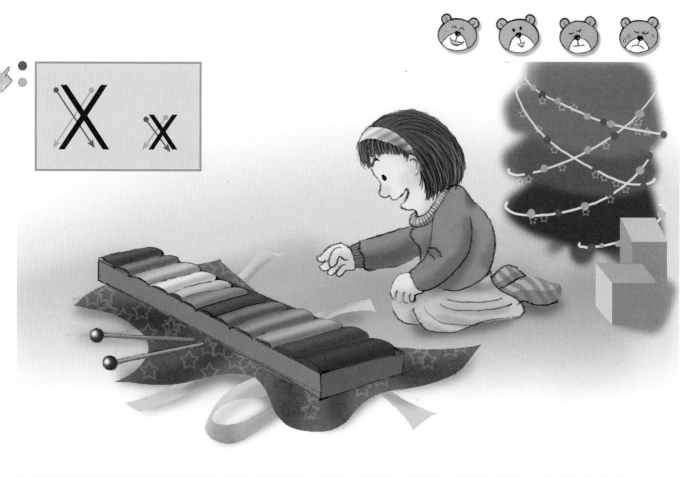

# X x

My X'mas gift is a xylophone.

My X'mas gift is a xylophone.

My X'mas gift is a xylophone.

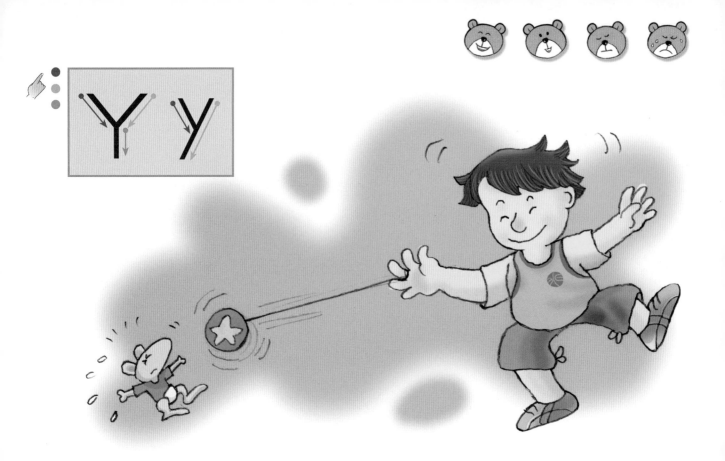

The young boy is playing yo-yo.

The young boy is playing yo-yo.

The young boy is playing yo-yo.

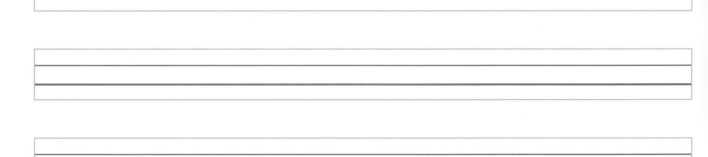

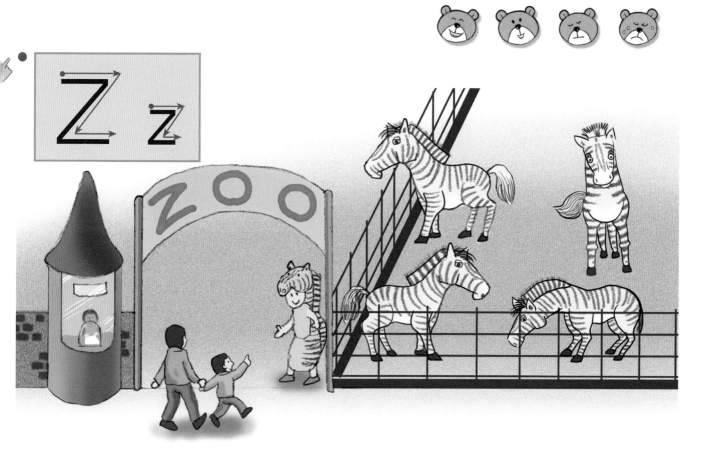

There are four zebras in the zoo.

There are four zebras in the zoo.

There are four zebras in the zoo.

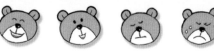

 請填上正確的顏色。
Colour the pictures.

🔴 red

🟡 yellow

🟤 brown

⚪ white

🟠 orange

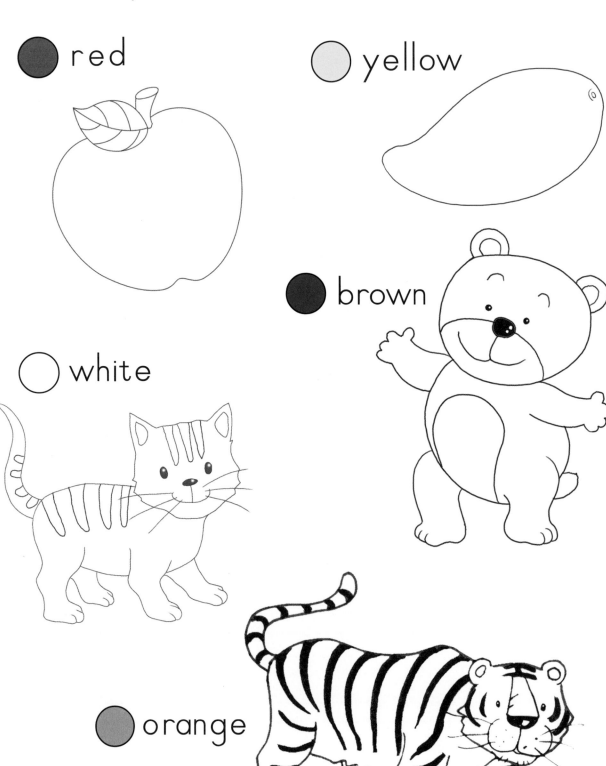

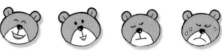

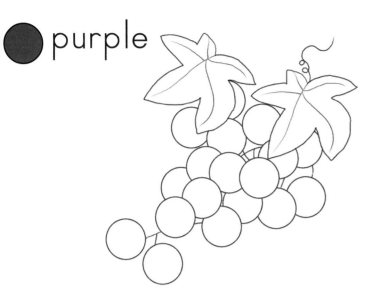

purple

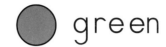

green

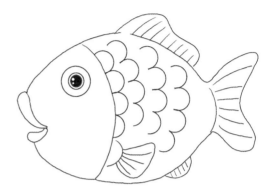

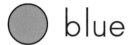

blue

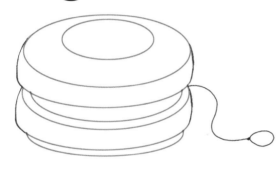

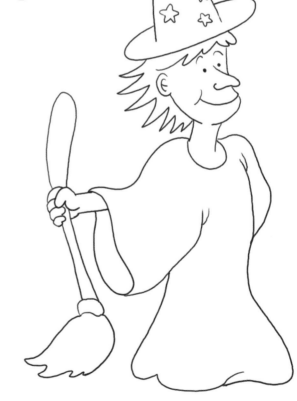

black

grey

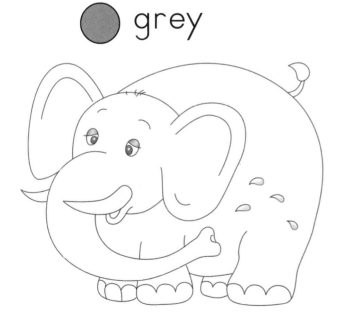

請填上缺少的字母。
Please fill in the missing letters.

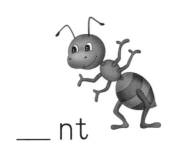
__ nt

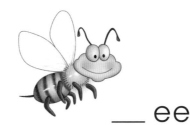
__ ee

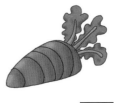
__ arrot

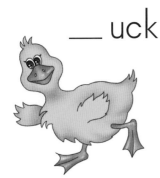
__ uck

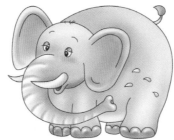
__ lephant

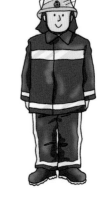
__ ireman

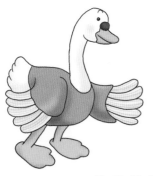
__ oose

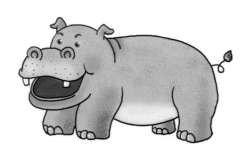
__ ippo

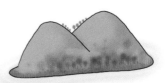
__ sland

__ ion

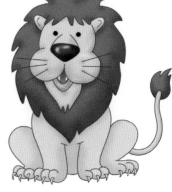

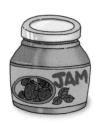
__ am

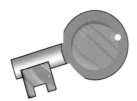
__ ey

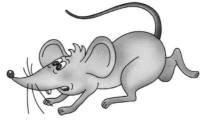
__ ouse

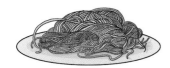
__oodles

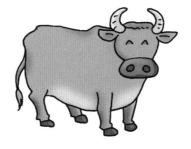
__ x

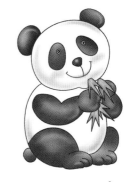
__anda

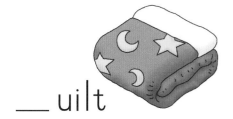
__uilt

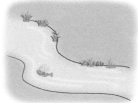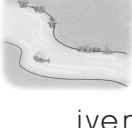
__iver

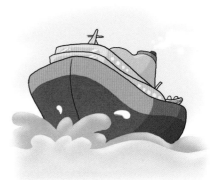
__hip

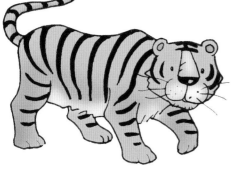
__iger

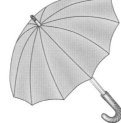
__mbrella

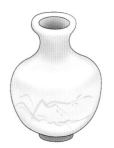
__ase

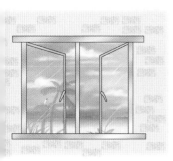
_indow

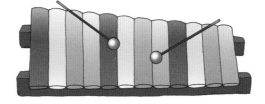
__ylophone

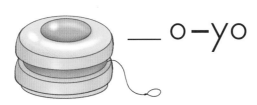
__o-yo

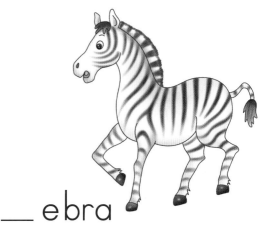
__ebra

請填上適當的字母。
Please fill in the missing letters.

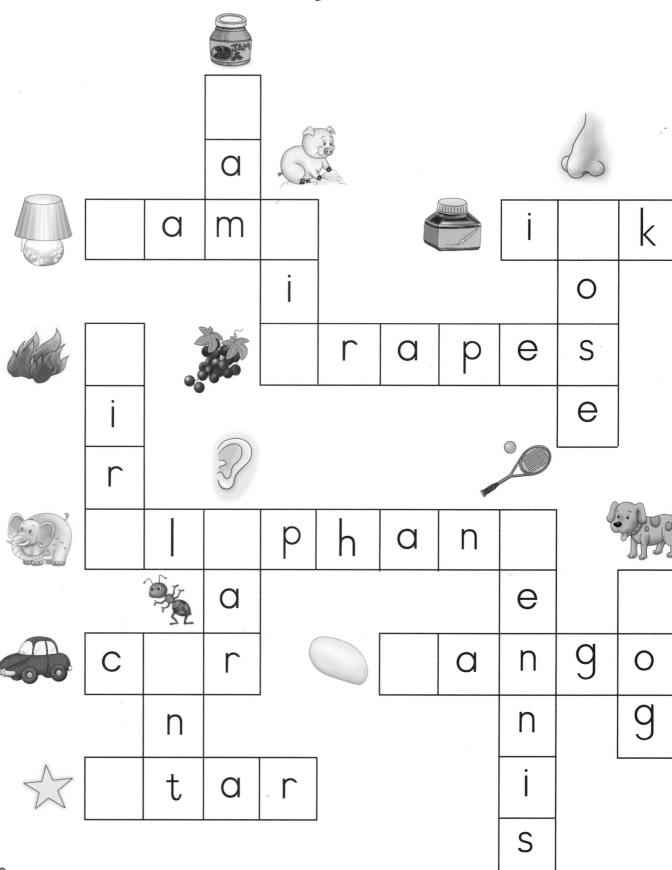